SOCIAL MEDIA
GUIDE FOR MINISTRY

NILS SMITH

Group resources really work!

This Group resource incorporates our R.E.A.L. approach to ministry. It reinforces a growing friendship with Jesus, encourages long-term learning, and results in life transformation, because it's:

Relational—Learner-to-learner interaction enhances learning and builds Christian friendships.

Experiential—What learners experience through discussion and action sticks with them up to 9 times longer than what they simply hear or read.

Applicable—The aim of Christian education is to equip learners to be both hearers and doers of God's Word.

Learner-based—Learners understand and retain more when the learning process takes into consideration how they learn best.

Social Media Guide for Ministry

Copyright © 2013 Nils Smith

Visit our website | group.com

Editor: Sue Brage
Art Director: Amy Taylor
Assistant Editor: Ardeth Carlson

ISBN 978-0-7644-9889-3

Printed in the United States of America.

10 9 8 7 6 5 4 3 2   22 21 20 19 18 17 16 15 14 13

CONTENTS

FOREWORD

Jesus said to "Go into all the world and make disciples." Little did his disciples know, 2,000 years later Facebook and Twitter would be major tools used to accomplish this commission.

Nils Smith is our social media pastor at Community Bible Church, and I could not think of a better person to lead that ministry. Daily, he ministers to a worldwide audience as he sits quietly in front of his Mac. It still amazes me every time he sends me stories and testimonies from people all around the world that tell us how much Jesus has changed their life. And it was because of a simple tool called social media.

I know that your staff, volunteers, and leadership teams will greatly benefit from this book. Nils gives you all of the tools he has learned in a concise and easy-to-read format. I pray that you catch the excitement of social media—and the endless possibilities it offers us—to carry out the Great Commission faster and broader than ever before.

Chris Emmitt
Executive Pastor, Community Bible Church
San Antonio, Texas

INTRODUCTION:
HOW I GOT STARTED

Growing up, I never dreamed that one day I would become a social media pastor. I definitely did not see myself as a pastor, and social media did not even exist! As it turns out, though, it's my dream job!

I began doing youth ministry as a 19-year-old college student in 1999 and quickly found that I had two invaluable ministry tools at my disposal: a church van and AOL Instant Messenger. I would drive the church van around Baytown, Texas, all day long, picking up students and building relationships with my students and their friends. However, those relationships were often just at a surface level—until we would begin chatting on Instant Messenger that evening.

I began strategically using Instant Messenger as a way to engage students and their friends in ways we never could before. While I quickly saw the danger in this ministry, more than anything else I saw the opportunity.

That summer, I saw dozens of students accept Christ, not because of the technology but through the power of the Gospel being communicated through the technology.

This was just the beginning of social media ministry; and as technology has continued to change, so has the world around us and so has the way that we utilize this technology. Ten years ago my online ministry consisted of chatting with 10 to 20 teenagers on Instant Messenger on a regular basis.

Today, I oversee a Facebook page (facebook.com/cbconline) with 200,000 fans from across the world, and our online worship gatherings touch over 10,000 people each week from over 100 countries, in both English and Spanish. We respond to 20 to 40 prayer requests each day, as well as 10 to 20 people indicating a decision to accept Christ every week. These results in a short year and a half were made possible through social media.

The world around us is changing rapidly, and social media is truly a game changer when it comes to ministry. I hope you will join me on this exciting journey as we focus on the opportunity in front of us to maximize ministry efforts through these online resources.

WHY SOCIAL MEDIA IS IMPORTANT TO YOUR MINISTRY

So what is social media, anyway? It is just what its name suggests: media that is social. Social media is an ongoing conversation on the Internet, with new conversations beginning every time someone makes a new post. People share content (status updates, video uploads, photos, and so on), and the social interaction begins.

When you post a video, article, church event, or any type of content on a social network, you are initiating a conversation. People can then Like, Comment, Share, or ignore your post. This interactive element completely changes the game when it comes to church communication.

The impact of technology is nothing new to the church. The ministry of the church has been transformed many times over in the past 2,000 years, due to technological advancements. Think about the printing press with the Bible or television and radio broadcasts for church services, sermons, and worship music. These were revolutionary in their time, just as social media is today.

Social media, like these previous technological advancements, allows the messages we communicate to go farther faster. It also allows everyone to interact with those messages. In the past, people might discuss a sermon over lunch, but today it's tweeted about as it's happening. The impact of this interaction is more powerful than we can imagine. So why should you use social media?

> *Jesus came and told his disciples, "I have been given all authority in heaven and on earth. Therefore, go and make disciples of all the nations, baptizing them in the name of the Father and the Son and the Holy Spirit. Teach these new disciples to obey all the commands I have given you. And be sure of this: I am with you always, even to the end of the age.* (Matthew 28:18-20)

We are called to share the love of Christ with all the world. Throughout history, I don't know if there has ever been a greater tool to do this than the Internet and, specifically, social media. We cannot take this opportunity lightly. While reaching people face-to-face can make a significant impact, that's simply not an option for everyone, and your reach can be very limited. What's important is that we reach out as much as possible, as often as possible, utilizing all means possible.

Take a minute to digest these statistics and points from Socialnomics.net* in 2012:

- If Facebook were a country, it would be the world's third largest and two times the size of the U.S. population.

- Over 50% of the world's population is under 30 years old.

- Social media has overtaken pornography as the number one activity on the Web.

- Facebook tops Google for weekly traffic in the U.S.

- Lady Gaga, Justin Bieber, and Britney Spears have more Twitter followers than the entire populations of North Korea, Australia, Chile, Israel, Sweden and Greece combined.

- A new member joins LinkedIn every second.

- The second-largest search engine in the world is YouTube.

- Because of the speed in which social media enables communication, word of mouth now becomes world of mouth.

- We don't have a choice on whether we *do* social media; the question is how *well* we do it.

- Social media isn't a fad; it's a fundamental shift in the way we communicate.

---

*socialnomics.net/2012/01/04/39-social-media-statistics-to-start-2012/

Before we get started, I want to discuss two *big* misunderstandings about social media that I often hear.

Social Media will make you relevant! This is wrong. Through the power of social networks, we are seeing the impact of many churches growing rapidly, while others are declining just as rapidly. Many ministry leaders have come to me asking for help using social media so their church might become relevant. The reality is that if you are not relevant in your local context, it is doubtful that you will be relevant online. The technology does not make you relevant, but it can make relevant messages more effective in reaching a greater potential audience.

Social Media is free! This is also incorrect. While Facebook, Twitter, and many of these other social networks do not have a financial cost, they still come with a cost—our time. It is impossible to effectively utilize social media without a great time investment. We don't simply communicate a message; we are joining a conversation and building relationships. These relationships require an investment of time and consistency. Trust me when I tell you that it's worth it!

When it comes to ministry, doesn't it all come down to relationships anyway? Our relationship with God and our relationships with others. Social media empowers us to build new relationships, even if they do look a little different than what we're used to.

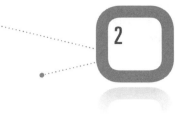

DISCOVERING YOUR SOCIAL MEDIA TOOLBOX

So let's get down to it. What are the basic tools that you need for your social media toolbox? I will highlight the "Big Five" social networks I think you need to be knowledgeable about, as well as three faith-based networks that I'm personally a fan of. I will also share some sites that I will give an honorable mention and think you should check out but aren't yet critical to your ministry.

Facebook (facebook.com)

How they describe themselves: Facebook's mission is to give people the power to share and make the world more open and connected.

Overview: Millions of people use Facebook every day to keep up with friends, upload an unlimited number of photos, share links and videos, and learn more about the people they meet.

What you need to know: There are over 900 million users (and growing) on Facebook from all over the world, and over half of those users log in daily. Active users range from early teenagers to senior citizens.

Who should use it: This is simple—everyone! Facebook has far-reaching mass appeal and functionality, making it a key tool for every ministry, no matter the demographic you are targeting.

How you should use it: There are a multitude of ways churches and ministries can use Facebook. I'll go into this in more depth in a later chapter.

Churches/ministries using Facebook effectively:

Jesus Daily (facebook.com/JesusDaily)

Pastor Joe Wood (facebook.com/pastorjoewoodfans)

Hillsong Church London (facebook.com/hillsongchurchlondon)

Ministry Story—Meeting Jim

Six months into launching CBC Online, I met an online participant named Jim. He shared with us in our live chat that he saw a Facebook status update for CBC Online and thought it was the Canadian Broadcast Channel. Even though it was not what he was looking for, the video captured his attention, and the community that he experienced engaged him. →

Jim quickly became an active participant in our online community and openly shared about his bitterness toward the Christian church that had developed over the years. He had not attended church since he was a teenager (Jim is now in his early 60's) and had deep scars from his negative experiences. Jim was captivated though by our community and quickly built friendships with our congregants through Facebook.

One morning when I got into the office, I received a Facebook message from Jim asking me if he could give me a call. I gave him my number, and we were on the phone within minutes. He wanted to know more about what it meant to accept Christ and if that meant he would have to go to a physical church again.

I answered all of Jim's questions and asked him if he was ready to make the decision to accept Christ as his Lord and Savior. He said he was not ready yet, but his heart was changing rapidly. Two weeks later Jim called me back, and his first words were: "Pastor Nils, I'm ready."

Today Jim is one of our strongest leaders at CBC Online, and his transformed life ministers to hundreds through his online ministry on Facebook.

Jim's life was transformed because of the power of the Gospel, but the Gospel was communicated through the technology of ➝

Facebook. It all began with a simple Facebook post. Who knows how God might use your next Facebook post?

Twitter (twitter.com)

How they describe themselves: The fastest, simplest way to stay close to everything you care about.

Overview: Twitter is a real-time information network that connects you to the latest stories, ideas, opinions, and news about what you find interesting. Simply find the accounts you find most compelling, and follow the conversations.

At the heart of Twitter are small bursts of information called Tweets. Each Tweet is 140 characters long, but don't let the small size fool you—you can discover a lot in a little space. You can see photos, videos, and conversations directly in Tweets to get the whole story at a glance and all in one place.

Hashtags—You might have heard about hashtags on TV or through other social networks. On any Twitter post, if you place the pound sign (#) before any word or combination of letters and numbers, this is called a hashtag. This allows you to easily search other postings on Twitter using the same hashtag. We use the hashtag #cbconline for anyone posting about CBC

Online to help others discussing CBC Online on Twitter to connect with each other. Here are some common ministry-related hashtags:

#kidmin and #cmconnect (children's ministry)

#stumin and #youthministry (youth ministry)

#collegemin (college ministry)

#churchmedia and #churchtech (church tech/media)

#church and #churches (general church)

#worship and #sundaysetlist (worship)

#missions (missions)

#pastor and #pastors (pastoral leadership)

#churchleadership and #leadership
(church leadership)

#churchplanting (church plants)

Search.twitter.com—This is one of the most powerful tools on the Internet! If you want to get the pulse about what is going on in your city or just join an already ongoing conversation, this is a great tool. Try searching for "I need prayer" or search the name of your city and see what others are saying. The possibilities related to this tool are endless.

Trending—Twitter pulls information from every post and lists the topics they see are being talked about the most. You will see this information listed as Trending Topics. These are often hashtags.

Retweet—When you see a tweet from someone that you follow, you can retweet it so that all of your followers can read it, as well. A great way to find new people to follow is to see who others are retweeting and follow them.

Direct Message—A direct message, often referred to as a "DM", is a private message between two Twitter users. This is like an e-mail or Facebook message but is also limited to 140 characters. You can only send a direct message to someone who follows you.

How you should use it: The most important thing you can do on Twitter is listen. Utilize search.twitter.com, and hear what people say about your ministry or in general about your city and community. Begin tweeting impactful messages that you believe will provide value to your followers, and always reply to anyone who directs a comment or question towards you. Retweet valuable posts from those in your ministry and tweets that you believe your followers will find of value.

Make sure to also monitor your time on Twitter, as the stream can pull you in and waste too much of your time. You will not be able to read every tweet, but read as many and reply to as many as you can.

Churches/ministries using Twitter effectively:

Rick Warren (twitter.com/RickWarren)

Woodlands Church (twitter.com/#!/woodlandschurch)

CharlotteONE (twitter.com/#!/CharlotteONE)

Hashtags are a great way to connect people around a specific topic or event. Create a hashtag (keep it short) of a combination of six to eight letters or numbers, and begin posting it for your church members to see on the screens, bulletin, and anywhere you can display it. Encourage your church to use it at the end of any tweet about the church or ministry.

Hashtags will not only create an outreach opportunity for the followers of your church members but also a way for your members to connect with each other. Members can begin to follow each other and not only share ministry highlights but also connect in a personal way, as well.

When creating hashtags for your church, I encourage you to avoid creating separate hashtags between ministries. Try using the one hashtag to unite all aspects of your church or ministry.

LinkedIn (LinkedIn.com)

How they describe themselves: Connect the world's professionals to make them more productive and successful.

Overview: LinkedIn is the world's largest professional network on the Internet, with more than 161 million members in over 200 countries and territories.

The LinkedIn website was launched in 2003 and currently counts executives from all Fortune 500 companies as members.

How you should use it: LinkedIn has two primary purposes for ministry leaders: 1) connecting with other pastors/ministry leaders; and 2) getting to know individuals in your congregation on a professional level. It might also provide valuable insights into skills they might have that are needed in the life of your church or ministry.

The most effective use I can suggest is to maximize groups. Create a group or multiple groups for your church members to connect on this network. Also connect in groups with other ministry leaders in similar ministry areas, and if you cannot find one, create one!

Ministry Story—Youth Pastors Group

Being in ministry can be very lonely, and connecting with other pastors can be critical to long-lasting ministry success. LinkedIn is primarily known as a resume-sharing site for those searching for a new job but can actually be a better resource for staying in your current ministry role rather than leaving it.

LinkedIn groups are an incredible way to network with other pastors with similar roles to yours. While I was serving in youth ministry, I randomly found a youth pastors group on LinkedIn and quickly jumped in. This group ⟶

became an incredible resource to me for ideas and inspiration from other youth pastors located across the country.

The most important thing this group provided me was community with peers in sharing my struggles, as well as hearing others' struggles. In this group we vented, we prayed, and we shared some of the funniest youth group stories you have ever heard! It was just what I needed.

The demands of ministry can often be very draining physically, emotionally, and spiritually. We need to experience community in ways that we often cannot in our local congregations. I encourage you to find or create a group on LinkedIn where you can also experience that community.

Churches/ministries/pastors using LinkedIn effectively:

Brandon Cox (linkedin.com/in/brandonacox)

Phil Thompson (linkedin.com/in/philthompsonlive)

Pastors Network (linkedin.com/groups/Pastors-Network-731467?gid=731467&mostPopular=&trk=tyah)

![You Tube] YouTube (YouTube.com)

How they describe themselves: YouTube provides a forum for people to connect, inform, and inspire others across the globe and acts as a distribution platform for original content creators and advertisers.

Overview: Founded in February 2005, YouTube allows billions of people to discover, watch, and share originally-created videos.

Who should use it: Any ministry interested in posting video content online should start with YouTube. Creating quality video content is becoming easier, cheaper, and more important. YouTube is the second largest search engine in the world and a great way to reach your audience with the searchability and shareability of these videos.

How you should use it: Upload your videos, title them creatively, and make sure to tag them effectively so they are easy to find. Don't stop using YouTube once the video is uploaded; make sure to respond when people comment on your videos, and continue the conversation.

One very popular reason that I hear about why people don't use YouTube is that they are nervous about what videos YouTube might recommend at the end of your video. I believe this is an even greater reason to use YouTube, as this network of video content needs more Christ-centered content to be recommended at the end of other videos.

! Ministry Tip—Using YouTube for Children's Ministry

Do you ever struggle to find a creative illustration for your weekly lesson in Sunday school or kids' church? YouTube is the second-largest search engine on the Internet (behind Google, who also owns YouTube) and is packed with creative content. This tip must come with a warning that you never know what you might find on YouTube. If you need something to stir the creativity inside you and search with discretion, YouTube is just the place. You will quickly go from *needing* an illustration to deciding *which* illustration to use.

Churches/ministries/pastors using YouTube effectively:

LifeChurch.tv (youtube.com/user/LifeChurchtv)

DJ Chuang (youtube.com/user/djchuang)

Elevation Worship (youtube.com/user/elevationworship)

Ministry Story—Family Moments With Sean Metcalf

One day I was talking with our children's pastor, Sean Metcalf, and asked if he wanted to shoot a quick video for families. I suggested that we post it to YouTube and see what would happen. He called it "A Family Moment with Sean Metcalf" and discussed the importance ⟶

of praying together as a family. It was basically a 3-minute sermon on video.

Shortly after recording the video, we posted it to YouTube and shared a link to it on Facebook and Twitter. Within a day, 300 people had watched the video, and still today dozens more watch the video each day. This sermon never dies on YouTube and, hopefully, will minister to thousands for years to come!

Sean has been able to share these videos with families in our local congregation, but the ministry touch will not end there! There are families all over the world that continue to find this video online, and it ministers to them where they are.

Videos on YouTube can be created in minutes using your smartphone or webcam, and the potential ministry impact is limitless. Be creative, and see what happens!

Pinterest (pinterest.com)

How they describe themselves: Pinterest is a Virtual Pinboard. Pinterest lets you organize and share photos of beautiful things you find on the Web. People use pinboards to plan their weddings, decorate their homes, and organize their favorite recipes. Best of all, you can browse pinboards created by other people. Browsing pinboards is a fun way to discover new things and get inspiration from people who share your interests.

Overview: Pinterest is the fastest-growing social network today and cannot be ignored. While the demographic is expanding rapidly when it comes to women's ministry, there is a huge opportunity to engage women who are spending hours on this site each week.

Ministry Tip—Women's Ministry

Creating content and posting inspirational messages can be very valuable in engaging women in your ministry online. This can also be very time-consuming and challenging without graphic designers to help you. You should not let a lack of content prevent you from being active on this rapidly growing social network.

Instead of worrying about creating new content on Pinterest, focus more on repinning the most valuable content you can find. Re-pin photo pins from the women in your ministry, and share things like parenting or organizing tips, Scriptures, inspirational quotes, home ideas, book recommendations, even recipes and healthy living tips! I think you will quickly find that great content already exists on the network, and your time will be best spent finding the best content to re-pin rather than creating new content to share.

Churches/ministries using Pinterest effectively:

Mars Hill Church Seattle (pinterest.com/marshill/)

Church Urban Fund (pinterest.com/churchurbanfund/pins/)

> **!** **Ministry Tip**—KidMin Creativity on a Budget
>
> Do your children's ministry classrooms need refreshing? Ever need a quick craft idea for Sunday? Pinterest is packed with creative ideas for any size budget! Simply go to Pinterest.com and search things such as "classroom ideas" or "craft activities." As you find creative ideas that you like, begin looking at the user's other pins, as well. You will likely find many other similar creative ideas that you can also use in your children's ministry.

MINISTRY-BASED NETWORKS

fv **FaithVillage** (FaithVillage.com)

How they describe themselves: FaithVillage is a social network of faith experiences designed around a virtual village that delivers a powerful, free social media platform for members, groups, and organizations with a robust publishing platform for Christian articles, blogs, videos, and audio. With both content and community, FaithVillage provides a safe, faith-friendly space for expanding personal faith, sharing ministry resources, and connecting with the causes you care about.

Overview: FaithVillage has a big vision that recently launched in beta phase at faithvillage.com. A quick scan of the village places reveals the breadth of content available here: leadership, Christian living, causes, faith & culture, art, video, podcasts, and more. As a shared publishing platform for Christ-followers, content is curated from contributors and content partners (bloggers, publishers, causes, churches, universities, church resource organizations); user-uploaded video, audio, and blogs; and original content from their editorial team. The social platform called The Lofts provides a personal networking space for members, private or public groups, and organizations that serves as a hub for all affiliated groups and content, such as for a church.

What you need to know: FaithVillage offers a wide range of great Christian content and community-building technology. It is a safe place to send your congregants for inspiration and leadership development, as you can trust the content and ads they will see. However, this is not a site that's best for outreach or people to engage their non-Christian friends. Though they may find helpful content here to share with friends as a way of introducing the Christian faith or ministering to them, it is a site that's best for cultivating discipleship and ministry skills and connecting people in Christian relationships.

! Ministry Tip—Bible Study Groups

FaithVillage is a great new social network where you never have to worry about offensive ads or negative content. Not only is it full of great content but also this robust site offers a social network just for the church. There have been other similar "Christian social networks," but they were not free, and they did not already have the great content already associated with the site.

You can easily set up a church or ministry page within the network (similar to a Facebook page), and within each page, you can set up groups for each ministry area, Sunday school class, or LifeGroup. These groups allow the community to stay connected throughout the week and send updates and reminders. Maximizing a network like this allows for community 24/7 rather than just the 1-hour a week that you might have in person.

Media Social (mediasocial.tv)

How they describe themselves: Media Social is a Facebook app that provides a broadcast social TV channel through the Internet.

What you need to know: I must admit that I have a bias toward this platform, as this is the online church platform we have used for CBC Online (OnlineChurch.com) since our launch. Its integration with Facebook and clean and simple functionality are incredible for both the ministry and end user. At a cost of $100 per month (including video streaming), this platform is second to none (ministry-based or not).

While the platform is robust in its functionality, it is incredibly easy for any church or ministry to use and even easier for the end user. You simply upload any videos that you have on file and schedule them for viewing. These can be sermons, Bible studies, training videos, or really any video content that you would like to share. Your viewers can watch the video together while also chatting on the Livewall with each other through their Facebook credentials, take notes, see a map of where everyone is from, and so much more. This really is the perfect solution for any ministry that is interested in launching online church services or online LifeGroups/Bible studies.

Ministry Story—Thank You, Pastor

> A couple months ago I was standing at a booth in our atrium at Community Bible Church, representing CBC Online. A gentleman walked up to me and said, "I just wanted to say thank you, pastor, and shake your hand." He continued, "You probably don't remember me, but I was the soldier in Afghanistan that used to log in about a year ago." ⟶

How could I forget! He would log in to CBC Online while he was stationed in Afghanistan, and so would his family here in San Antonio, Texas. They would all log in at the same time so they could all worship together as a family. It was such a special moment each week to see their family interact and their gratefulness to the technology that made this possible.

They were always so thankful to me for offering the opportunity to worship together, but I was the one thankful to Media Social for developing this technology that makes all of this possible. All I did was upload and schedule a video.

YouVersion (YouVersion.com)

How they describe themselves: YouVersion represents a new frontier from LifeChurch.tv. According to the site, they aren't just building a tool to impact the world using innovative technology; they are engaging people in relationships with God as they discover the relevance the Bible has for their lives.

What you need to know: This Web application is so much more than just a text Bible or just a social network. LifeChurch.tv created such an incredible tool for people to read and interact with the Bible with others.

One of the great tools built into this app is the Live Events tool. The live events feature serves as a digital bulletin for participants to take notes, share to social networks, give online, and so much more. No more picking up paper bulletins after church, and you know this bulletin is going home with your church members!

The Reading Plans feature is also a great tool that can be used to encourage your congregation to read the Bible in a structured way. It gives users a reminder if they are behind or encouragement in how to pace their reading. There is a great variety of plans for new believers, as well as for deep theologians.

Ministry Tip—Adult Ministry

Have you begun to notice how many people are now using their smartphones to read the Bible in church? Well actually, to read their Bible, period! You can make it even easier for them as well as giving them other important information by utilizing the YouVersion Live Events tool.

You can quickly create a "digital bulletin" in this feature, allowing members to pull up news, info, sermon notes, Scripture passages; find online giving options; share prayer requests; and so much more!

These live events can be created in minutes and can be used for not just worship services but also Sunday school classes, Bible studies, special events, or any gathering of people ⟶

revolving around studying the Bible. People can find your event either by searching for a title or based on your geographic location.

Give it a try, and see what your congregation thinks. At a cost of FREE, the only risk you are taking is losing the 15 minutes of time that it will take you to set it up!

Honorable Mention

g+ Google+ (plus.google.com)

This is an interesting platform primarily because it's tied to Google. It is great for information that you want to be searchable. Google+ hangouts are a pretty cool feature, but the user base isn't large enough to make it worth the investment at this point. However, it's worth keeping an eye on and setting up a basic profile for yourself and a page for you ministry.

! Ministry Tip—Leader Training

Google+ does not have mass appeal (yet), but it does have some unique functionality. One of the most attractive features of Google+ is the hangouts where you can have a group video chat, screen share (show a slide show for everyone to see), or watch a YouTube video together. ➡

Do you ever want to gather your leaders, but busy schedules make this difficult? Try using a Google hangout for your next leader training. You can create a PowerPoint slide show to display through the screen share feature and have Q&A through the video chat functionality.

One of the other great features of Google hangouts is that they can be recorded simply and instantly be uploaded to YouTube with one-click immediately following your session. Then leaders who may have missed the training can watch the YouTube video and still get the information they need.

Blogging platforms

 Wordpress (wordpress.com)

Blogspot (blogspot.com)

Tumblr (tumblr.com)

These blogging platforms are available in a free version or self-hosted for more customization. Wordpress seems to be more popular, while Blogspot has a lot of value because it's connected to Google and is very easy to use. Tumblr is the new kid on the block and seems to be the "trendy" blogging platform at the moment.

Ministry Story—The Kisers' Blog

My sister was a very active Bible study teacher for many years and was sad to have to step away from teaching weekly after having her first child. She is passionate about ministering to women, but her family must come first, and the commitment of teaching a weekly Bible study was too much with her busy schedule.

While she stepped away from teaching in a Sunday school classroom each week, she did not step away from ministering to a community of ladies. She became very active on her personal blog (thekisers.blogspot.com), sharing life and speaking truth into the ladies who read her blog. Her ministry impact on the blog does not stop in her posts, as she is also able to interact with her readers through comments around each post.

On average 300 to 500 different ladies read each post that Becky puts up on her blog. That's quite a ministry opportunity that she's able to have while blogging during naptime! She's also reaching many women that could never have attended her Bible study due to distance or time.

Instagram (instagram.com)

Have you noticed that we use our smartphones to do a lot more than talk on the phone? I think our smartphones could actually be better described as smart cameras that can also be used as a computer and phone in your pocket. People love to both share photos and see photos!

Instagram has created a very simple social network that integrates easily with Twitter and Facebook as well as sharing photos between friends. Instagram has grown rapidly and was recently purchased by Facebook, making it even more interesting to watch how it develops in the future. The initial attraction to Instagram for most users is the filters you can add to any of your photographs, instantly making an average photo look like a masterpiece, but it is the social network that keeps them engaged.

Ministry Tip—Smartphone Photographers

Remember when you used to check out the church camera and designate an "event photographer"? Now everyone with smartphones can serve as your event photographers, and Instagram gives you a platform to instantly share those photographs, as well. You might try having some unofficial contests of who can take the best picture at an event or pick out a couple of pictures to post on your ministry website or Facebook page. ⟶

Another great way to encourage your congregants in using Instagram is to document with their photos where they see God throughout the week. Those photos will likely include sunsets and nature but might also portray things like people and places. A picture can truly speak a thousand words.

Video Streaming

Livestream (livestream.com)

U-Stream (ustream.com)

With either of these platforms, you can literally begin streaming live video today for free through your smartphone, webcam, or a camera you connect to your computer. It will amaze you how easy it is today for anyone to broadcast a live event online. My first experience with Online Church came through live streaming our college ministry service through Livestream.com. It was very easy, and we simply shared a link on the screens for everyone in the room to invite friends on Facebook or Twitter. Instantly we had dozens joining us through this free streaming service.

There are many possibilities with these sites, but unless you want to pay significantly more, your viewers will see ads that you are unable to control. This is a great starting point for any ministry interested in experimenting with live streaming video.

Ministry Tip—Broadcasting Kids' Camp

The most effective use that I found with the free service Live Stream was when we experimented with broadcasting our camp services online for parents to log in and hear the messages that their kids were hearing. Parents loved hearing what their children were learning and getting a taste of what their kids were experiencing. For that purpose, the quality was not as important as the opportunity to share the content.

You can broadcast easily with your iPhone or webcam and be online instantly. You can also get more high tech by connecting a camera and audio signal through the soundboard to your computer. This is a simple solution that can allow parents or anyone in your church to experience camp alongside your ministry.

Church Online Platform (churchonlineplatform.com)

Streaming Church (streamingchurch.tv)

Church Online Platform is the platform used by LifeChurch.tv and is offered to churches at no cost. You will need to pay for video streaming, or you can integrate U-Stream or Livestream into this platform.

Streaming Church is a paid platform but is an all-in-one system, with live streaming capabilities at a very affordable price.

FourSquare (foursquare.com)

This is a very cool location-based check-in network that has become less relevant due to the new Facebook Places function in Facebook. Encouraging people to "check-in" while at your church as well as leaving tips and comments about your church for others to see can be a great outreach opportunity.

Hootsuite (hootsuite.com)

Tweetdeck (tweetdeck.com)

Neither of these sites is a social network; they are tools used to manage all of your social networks in one place. One of the best features associated with these sites is the ability to preschedule posts to multiple social networks. Consider setting a day or time that you can create and schedule 5 to 10 posts for the week so you don't feel the need to post one day just because you had not yet posted.

THE FACEBOOK GUIDE

After that last chapter, you can see that there are a lot of tools in the social media toolbox, and it can quickly become overwhelming to a busy pastor or ministry leader. It's my recommendation that you start with Facebook before anything else.

While social media extends far beyond Facebook, understanding the ins and outs of this social network is critical. Many of the other sites have a central focus: YouTube for videos; Pinterest for pictures; and Twitter for short, mass, instant messaging. Facebook is in many ways an all-in-one network for individuals and organizations, with live text and video chat, inbox messages, wall posts, picture and video uploads, event invites, and so much more.

Many describe Facebook as being in a constant state of beta. This basically means that you should never get too comfortable, as it is always changing. While it does not always feel this way at the time, the changes are almost always making Facebook better. In maximizing Facebook, you must always remain flexible in your understanding and your approach.

In the following information I will describe many of the primary features of Facebook and their intended use.

Profile—This is the core of Facebook, where you represent yourself. You share your interests and basic personal information. One of the most important aspects to your profile is the profile picture, which is the image that is displayed next to every post you make. I generally encourage that you use a head shot or photo that represents you well.

One of the newest features on Facebook relates to the profile, as it is now created as a timeline. This functionality lays out your posts on a literal timeline, and you can add photos and life events on your personal timeline. Facebook really sees each individual's profile as an online scrapbook to document your life.

Personal Story—I'm Quitting Facebook

It literally took me years to convince my grandfather to join Facebook. When I showed him how he could stay connected with his kids, grandkids, and even great grandkids, he finally gave in. We set up an account for him, and he seemed to enjoy it for about a week. ➝

Then I got a call saying "I'm quitting Facebook." When I asked why, his response was, "Because I don't want people to get my bank account information." While this is funny to many, it is a very real concern for some.

The reality of Facebook is that people will only see what you share. If you do not want them to know your bank account information, don't post it. (By the way, no one should post their bank information.) This also goes for your address, phone number, e-mail address, pictures, work info, and so on. When it comes to filling out your profile, share what you want to share, and keep the rest private.

Groups—This is a great feature of Facebook that I recommend for life groups, Bible studies, ministry teams, or any small group within your church. Facebook describes these as a place to share things with the people who will care the most.

Groups are generally good when you don't envision the community growing to more than 100 people. One of the key advantages to these groups is that they can be public (anyone can join and participate); private (anyone can see and request to join but cannot see the conversations until accepted into the group); or secret (no one can see that the group exists unless they are invited).

Some of the groups that I am actively a part of:

- My personal LifeGroup—We have a Facebook group for our LifeGroup to interact throughout the week with reminders, prayer requests, etc.

- CBC Online ministry leaders—we have a group for all of our leaders to connect and learn from each other and keep each other updated on various situations regarding CBC Online.

- Online church practitioners—This is a group of other Online Church leaders who share resources and ideas and encourage each other in ministry

Ministry Tip—Adult Ministry

Are you finding that e-mail blasts for your Sunday school class or Bible study just don't work as well as they used to? Try setting up a Facebook group in replacement or in addition to your e-mail blasts. Groups are a great place for reminders as well as simply sharing life and for group members to connect with each other individually on Facebook.

It will only take you a few minutes to set up the group, and then you can easily add any of your current Facebook friends. For those with whom you are not already connected on Facebook, you can e-mail a link to the group to your current e-mail list. These groups are not just a great place for information sharing but also for sharing life events and prayer needs.

Pages—This is one of the most important tools that Facebook offers churches and ministries. Pages can be highly customized and should become a priority for your church or ministry to develop. Facebook offers great insights and flexibility for page owners to manage their pages as they choose. It's my belief that a church or ministry's Facebook page is just as important if not more important than their website.

Here are some of the most effective ministry Facebook Pages that I have found:

I Am Second (facebook.com/iam2nd)

CBC Online (facebook.com/CBConline)

Hillsong Church London (facebook.com/hillsongchurchlondon)

Jesus Daily (facebook.com/JesusDaily)

LifeChurch.tv (facebook.com/lifechurchtv)

Relevant Magazine (facebook.com/relevant)

Mars Hill Church (facebook.com/marshillchurch)

Ministry Tip—When Do You Meet?

One of the biggest mistakes churches make on their websites is not making it clear what time they meet/gather. This is true also for your Facebook page. People are often looking for the where and when while they visit your page, and they should not have to look hard for this. Be sure you make these times very visible in one or several places on your Facebook page.

News Feed—This feature was the primary game changer for Facebook when it was developed and is still the bread and butter for people to see what is going on. When you post content, it is primarily seen in the news feed, not on your page or profile. This is determined by Facebook's algorithm that is determined by how valuable they deem your content to be, based on interactions with your post. Strive for interactions (likes, comments, and shares), and this will lead to a greater number of impressions (how many people see your post).

Photos—Everyone loves pictures, and photos have always been an important part of Facebook. Sharing photos and tagging individuals is a great way for people to find your page, as well as for people to get to know your community before even visiting your church or ministry.

Videos—Videos have the highest impressions-to-interactions rate and draw the most attention. I would encourage you to upload videos to YouTube and post the link to the video on Facebook. YouTube videos can still be viewed without leaving Facebook and help build your traffic within both networks. Quality content is always more important than quality production, so don't let the lack of equipment limit you. Videos shot with your smartphone or webcam can be very effective.

Events—Basically the Facebook version of an e-vite, Events is a great tool for special church events or services (such as Easter or Christmas Eve). It is a great and easy-to-use evangelism tool for people to invite others to be a part of your ministry. It is also currently the only way to message a group of people within Facebook, as you can send a message to everyone who has been invited to an event or just those who have RSVP'd.

Ministry Tip—Women's Ministry

Do you have a women's ministry dinner or special event coming up? The Event feature is a great way to invite all of the women in your ministry that you are Facebook friends with, as well as creating an easy way for women to invite their friends, too. As your event gets closer, you can then send a message with important information about the event to those who have RSVP'd. You can also send a reminder message to those who have not responded. This is a tool that should be maximized for every special event in the life of your church or ministry.

Places (check in)—This feature is becoming more popular and is a cool way for people to let their friends know that they are at church or attending another ministry event. It's important to have your address listed on your page in a way that allows people to "check in" to your location, which then allows their friends to see where they are. Encourage your congregation and staff to check in to help promote the church and also see other church members who have checked in.

Birthdays—Everyone loves to get birthday greetings, especially from that unexpected person whom they greatly respect. Facebook makes it very easy for ministry leaders to simply spend 5 minutes a day to quickly see who is having a birthday and to comment on that person's wall. To really stand out, say something unique to that person as opposed to just "Happy Birthday."

Subscribe—This is one of Facebook's newest features and really helps to maximize your newsfeed. Without unfriending someone, you can now choose to limit or block (unsubscribe) someone from your newsfeed or choose to see only what Facebook deems as very important. If you find yourself annoyed by an over-poster on Facebook, don't hesitate to unsubscribe. (They won't know that you did!)

Security—Facebook offers a wide range of security features that allows you to keep your content very private or public, as you feel most comfortable. Make sure to check your profile security settings, and set them in a way that feels appropriate to you. Maximizing these security features can help you to really enjoy the network without worrying about who is seeing what.

Tagging—When posting a comment about a friend or sharing a picture of someone, you can tag them by typing the @ symbol and their name. The picture or comment will then be posted on their profile, as well. TIP: Be sure to use their Facebook "handle," which might be different from their name, if you want it to show up on their timeline.

Notes—This is a great feature that can be used very similarly to a blog. This is a good place to post written testimonies or sermon notes. People can then share these posts or comment and interact with them.

URL—One of the most valuable things you can have for your ministry Facebook page is an easy-to-remember URL. This would be the facebook.com/xxxx (whatever name you choose). You can go to facebook.com/username to secure your custom URL.

Spam—You don't want to see spam, and Facebook wants to protect you and their users from seeing these kind of messages. When you see inappropriate messages, do not hesitate to mark them as spam or block that individual. (Simply click on the small arrow at the top right corner of the post, and choose "Report Story" or "Spam.") The poster will not know who did this, and it really makes Facebook better for everyone.

For more Facebook basics, visit: facebook.com/help/basics

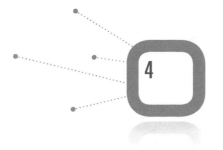

GETTING STARTED:
BABY STEPS

With all of these networks and so many options, it is hard to even know where to begin. So where should you start, and what should you do? Let me encourage you to start by taking baby steps and expand slowly as you become more comfortable online. Social media is much like any other new practice that you begin, and you do not want to overwhelm yourself by diving in too quickly.

Here are some very practical first steps.

STEP 1: SET UP A FACEBOOK ACCOUNT.

If you haven't already done this, do this now! Seriously, stop reading this book and go to facebook.com and set up an account. Facebook is king when it comes to the social networks, and it's the best place to start.

Take about 10 minutes to upload a photo and some basic information. You will be able to change and add information later, but get the basics up for your friends to know who you are.

If doing this sounds intimidating to you, don't be scared. If my mom can set up a Facebook account, anyone can. (No offense, Mom!) Facebook does a good job of walking you through the first steps in getting started. If you ever get confused, do what my IT (Information Technology) brother-in-law suggests—just Google your questions. You don't have to have a degree in computer science to figure this out, I promise.

STEP 2: ADD SOME FRIENDS.

You don't need hundreds of friends; just choose 15 to 20 of your friends and add them as Facebook friends. Again, Facebook will guide you through this as you set up your account.

STEP 3: LISTEN.

Watch the news feed. Read what your friends are sharing. Check out their profiles, and find out more about your friends and family than you ever knew. How long should you listen? My suggestion: every day for at least 15 minutes for two weeks.

Listening is the most important thing that you will do on social media, so it's important that you learn how to do this well before posting anything. For the first two weeks, I would encourage you to do nothing more than listening and liking various posts. Easy enough, right?

STEP 4: RESPOND.

Take baby steps when you begin interacting. Before creating a conversation, join existing conversations. As you feel comfortable, begin commenting on your friends' posts. This is a great way to affirm people or encourage them.

STEP 5: SHARE.

It's your turn to begin a conversation. Begin to think about what's going on in your life that you want to share with your friends and family. Do you feel like you don't have anything to share? If you're a follower of Christ, you have plenty to share.

Before you begin posting, though, please read the rest of this book. I will be sharing with you many of the mistakes and successes I have experienced myself or with others when sharing on Facebook or any other social network.

STEP 6: BRANCH OUT.

Do you feel comfortable with Facebook? Try branching out with one of the other many social networks (such as Twitter, LinkedIn, Pinterest, and Faith Village).

> **⚠ Ministry Tip**—Networks for Ministry
>
> Here are some networks I would focus on based on ministry area:
>
> Women—Pinterest
>
> Youth—Instagram
>
> Men/Women—LinkedIn
>
> College/Young Adult—Twitter
>
> Children/Family—YouTube
>
> Small Group—FaithVillage
>
> Worship—YouTube

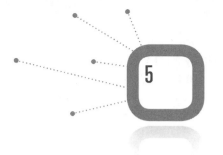

CREATING A CONVERSATION

So what should you post on Facebook? I can't give you an exact answer to this, and I don't think you should listen to anyone who tries to tell you they can. This is your platform, your voice, and your choice of what to post.

Remember that when you post to a social network, you are initiating a conversation. You are not just posting something for people to read; you are posting something for people to Like, Comment, or Share.

If you want more people to see your post, the key is getting into the news feed. You get into the news feed of your friends or fans through Facebook's algorithm that is based on how many people have liked, commented on, or shared your post. So if you have content that you want many people to see, you need to make sure it is social.

With that said, I don't want to tell you what to post, but I do want to share with you my experience with what we have done at Community Bible Church with the CBC Online Facebook page (facebook.com/cbconline). We have three types of posts that we typically rotate through:

- Inspiration—We post sermon points, Scripture verses, or song lyrics. Our hope in these posts is that people will "Like" these messages.

- Information—These posts are generally announcements about upcoming events, links, or some other piece of information that we want to share with our congregation. Our hope in posting information is that people will "Share" it with their friends. We have found that adding pictures to these posts help to make them much more appealing.

- Conversation—We simply ask a question. Sometimes it relates to a sermon series, and sometimes it's just about the weather. Our hope in asking a question is that people will "Comment," and that these posts will create a conversation. We believe these to be our most important posts, as conversations help build the community.

> **!** **Ministry Tip**—Can I Pray for You?
>
> As I think through our most successful posts on the CBC Online Facebook page, there is one post that we make at a different time each week that has proven to be more effective than any other: "How can we pray for you today?" ⟶

The requests we hear in response are often very heavy and things that we would not be aware of had we not asked. We pray for these individuals, and we follow up with many of them, as well. These responses have also been very valuable for our preaching pastors in having a pulse on what is going on in the lives of members of the congregation.

Here is one last tip. My friend Dr. Aaron Tabor created the Jesus Daily Facebook page (facebook.com/JesusDaily) that today has over 14 million fans from all over the world. I asked him if he could share with me any advice about growing a Facebook community. His tip was simple: "Ask them to do what you want them to do."

If you want them to like a comment, ask them to like it. If you want them to comment, ask them to comment. It sounds elementary, but don't we do the same thing in our worship services? Sometimes we're unsure whether we should sit or stand, but all we need is for the worship leader to lead us and tell us what to do (even if it seems obvious).

Disclaimer: Please don't presume that the number of comments, shares, retweets, and likes are an accurate reflection of the influence you are having. People still see what you have to share. You still have an influence regardless of the received responses. But yes, we do want to create a conversation to have a great influence.

MAXIMIZING YOUR TOOLS

STRATEGY AND GOALS

It is my opinion that most people overthink their strategy, so I don't want you to do that. But it is important to think through your organization and what your goals are. Set a strategy for how often you will post, what various types of content you will share, and some growth metrics that you desire to reach.

I would suggest that you set aside 15 minutes a week to review the insights from the past week and one hour a month to analyze the past month and restructure your strategy and goals for the coming month. A great tool that you can use in measuring social media growth is a website called Sparkwise. You can set up a free account at sparkwi.se.

Remember to set realistic goals. Social media moves fast, so you can easily get lost in it for hours. Put limits on yourself as you get started, and set realistic goals for posting and interactions.

LINKING NETWORKS

I have some good news! You don't have to update every social network with each message you post. Many of your social networks can automatically update each other.

For instance, when I update my LinkedIn account, I have it set to automatically update Twitter. In turn, Twitter automatically updates Facebook. I also have my YouTube videos and blog posts set to automatically update Twitter, which again automatically updates Facebook, as well.

Sound confusing? It's really not. Here are some step-by-step instructions on linking networks together.

Have your Twitter account update your Facebook profile:

1. Make sure you are logged in to both your Twitter and Facebook accounts.

2. Go to apps.facebook.com/twitter/.

3. Click on "Go to your Twitter Profile Settings to start."

4. Scroll down to the button that says "Post your Tweets to Facebook."

Have your Facebook page update your Twitter account:

1. Log in to your Twitter account, and go to your Facebook page.

2. Click on "Edit Page" and choose "Update Info."

3. Select "Resources" on the left-hand side, and choose "Link your Page to Twitter."

4. Choose the page, and then click "Link to Twitter."

5. Click the "Authorize App" button, and your Facebook page updates now update your Twitter account.

Update your Twitter account through LinkedIn:

1. Login to both your Twitter account and LinkedIn account.

2. In LinkedIn, go to "Profile" and "Edit Profile."

3. Scroll down to Twitter and click "Edit" and "Add a Twitter account."

4. Click the "Authorize App" button, and your LinkedIn posts will now be displayed on your Twitter account.

Display your Pinterest updates on Facebook:

1. Log in to both Facebook and Pinterest.

2. While in Pinterest, click on "Settings" and choose the option "Link to Facebook."

3. You will get a pop-up that says "Log in to Facebook." Select this button.

4. Go back into Pinterest settings, and there will now be an option to "Add Pinterest to Facebook Timeline," which you will want to check, as well as an option to "Find Facebook Friends on Pinterest,"

Updating Twitter and Facebook with YouTube:

1. Log in to Facebook, Twitter, and YouTube.

2. While on YouTube, choose "Settings" and then "Sharing."

3. Click on the "Connect" button next to Twitter, and then click to "Authorize App."

4. Click on the "Connect" button next to Facebook, and then click on the "Go to App" button.

5. You can now choose, under the "Share Your Activity" options, which activities you would like to share to these connected accounts.

When it comes to CBC Online, we simply use Facebook to update Twitter. On my personal accounts, I use a different combination. Know that there are all kinds of configurations that are possible and useful, based on your strategy, and there really is no right or wrong way to link networks. As you begin to expand to various sites, begin looking for ways to use the features to save time in keeping them all updated.

One thing to remember in expanding to multiple networks is that while you are able to easily post on multiple networks at once, they all should be monitored, as each post creates a new conversation on each site.

ASK GOOGLE

People often ask me if certain things are possible through social media or how to do things on various social networks. The first thing I do when I receive these questions is to do an internet search using a search engine like Google, Bing, or your favorite search site. You can skip a step in asking me or someone else most of your questions by simply searching on your own. It is amazing what you will find!

TOP SOCIAL
MEDIA MISTAKES

Anytime you try new things, you will make mistakes. It is my hope to help you avoid some of the mistakes that I have made or that I have seen others make. Don't worry too much about making mistakes, but be sure you learn from them so you make the most of your time online.

As I think through some of the mistakes I've made using social media, the CBC Online Facebook page stands out. I created the page with one goal in mind: to get people to link over to our Online Church site. I simply tried to get as many people to "Like" the page, and then I spammed them with many variations of the same post, asking them to click our link.

Not only did they not link over to the site but also many "Unliked" our page, as we were very annoying. This kind of marketing might work in mass mailers or even e-mail marketing but not on social media. I needed to provide valuable content and create a conversation, not just blast out a message.

Today our page has over 200,000 fans and is growing at a rate of almost 500 daily new likes since adjusting our strategy. In adjusting our strategy, we now only invite them to link over to Online Church in about 10% of our posts.

Here are some other mistakes that either I have made or have seen others make when using Social Media either as an individual or an organization:

Negativity—It's okay to share a complaint or two about a restaurant or business if you have a bad experience that you want your friends to avoid, but no one likes to hear the constant complainer.

TMI (Too Much Information)—Your friends don't want to hear about all of the details of your illness or every ingredient in the meal you just ate.

Politics/Agendas—This is your platform to share what you choose, but it can be a big turnoff when someone continues to share political agendas online. It is also important to remember that as a ministry leader, you are representing your church or ministry in everything you share online.

All Communication, No Conversation—Remember that you are creating a conversation. Social media is not just a place to shout about your upcoming events or blog posts. Try following the system each time you log in to listen (read) first, comment/like second, and post last.

All Professional, Never Personal—People want to see your pictures, hear about your passions, and know what's going on in your life both professionally and personally. You don't have to share every detail of your life, but make sure you share your own personality and personal interests, too.

!) Ministry Tip—Internal Communication

If you haven't already, use this chapter as a guide to discuss social media usage with your team. Talk about your expectations. Create some guidelines as a team as to what is acceptable or not, and agree to be accountable to one another. Often mistakes are made simply because someone didn't think. Setting up your expectations as a team can help everyone feel more confident and prevent problems.

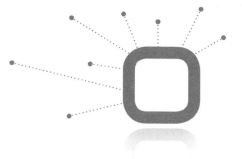

FREQUENTLY ASKED QUESTIONS

Q I don't have time for social media, but it seems important; what do I do?

Do just what you do for anything else in your life: Schedule your time wisely. Make sure to spend enough time using these tools but not too much time, letting it consume you.

Q I started with Facebook, but where should I go next?

That's up to you and your target audience. If you are involved in women's ministry, I would look to jump into Pinterest. If you are focused on young adults, you might try Twitter next. My personal preference would be YouTube, as I feel that web video is very important and will only continue to be more important in the future.

Q What happened to MySpace? Am I going to invest in these other social networks and then see them crash like MySpace did?

It is doubtful that Facebook will crash like MySpace did, as it has such a diverse user base. At the same time, in the world of technology, things change fast, and you really never know. The good news is that MySpace died because Facebook was better. If something else (such as Google+) becomes better than Facebook, then this could happen, but if it does, know that the tools you have at your fingertips will be that much better, as well. Don't get too comfortable; change is coming, and we must constantly adapt!

Q Should I create a blog right away?

I would not start a blog immediately, but if you believe that you or someone on your team can commit to posting at least once a week, a blog has a lot of value. Blogs provide a great platform for daily or weekly devotionals that don't fit into a short Facebook post or Tweet. I would start using the Notes feature on Facebook, which is similar to a blog, and if you are able to keep this updated on a regular basis, begin to transition these long-form posts to a blog.

Q I see more and more people using cell phones in church; should we discourage or encourage this activity?

As a social media pastor, I love seeing cell phones in church! In fact, I highly encourage you to make sure that you have Wi-Fi available, as you are likely also seeing more iPads and tablets in church, as well. They are great reading devices for the Bible and taking notes. Why would you not want your congregation posting comments about your church with their friends on social networks? For many young adults, this level of interaction helps them have a higher level of focus on the message while in church.

Q How did you grow the CBC Online Facebook Page to 200,000 fans?

There have been two keys to the growth of our Facebook page: consistency and creativity. We have worked diligently to provide valuable content to our Facebook community and asked them to share that content. We have teams of people who have worked hard to keep our posts consistent (multiple posts each day) and engaging. There is no secret formula, but without these two keys, your page will not grow "accidentally" like you might hope.

Q How do I get a video to go viral?

This is one of the funniest and most frustrating questions I hear. My honest answer is: you can't. There are great videos that people have worked very hard to get out there and never gained traction. There are also some of the dumbest videos that you will ever see that go viral!

The key question that you should ask, though, is whether your video is worth sharing. If people share the video and their friends like it and they think it's worth sharing, your video might go viral. Don't count on it, but don't stop putting out high-quality and creative videos. You never know what will catch on!

Q I'm still really confused! What should I do?

First, try not to stress out! As I mentioned before, social media can feel overwhelming. Start small with realistic goals; but please start somewhere.

If you do still need help getting started, you have a couple of options. You can find a young adult or teenager in your church and ask them for help. They, in many ways, are the true experts in this field. Or you can contact me at nils@nilssmith.com, and we can set up a time to connect.

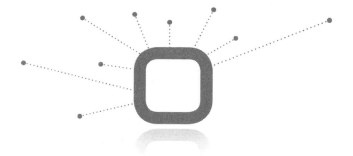

CONCLUSION

Social media is an incredible tool, but we must remember it is just that—a tool. Just as a sound system is an incredible tool to help our congregation hear better, it can also be a great distraction if not used effectively. If we spend too little time setting it up, sound checking, and making sure it's functioning properly, our message may not be heard. It's not the technology that's the issue; it just wasn't used effectively. On the flip side, we can spend so much time tweaking the system, making sure it functions correctly, that we don't spend time organizing our message. This is just as ineffective when it comes to communicating the Gospel.

Just like any other new technology or resource, social media has the opportunity to either enhance our ministry or quickly become a distraction. You must figure out for you and in your context how these tools can become a great asset to you and the teams that you lead.

Social media is quickly transforming the way we communicate and the culture around us. Business, politics, education, and religious beliefs are being shaped today through social media conversations. It is my opinion that this is not just a situation that we must respond to but, rather, an opportunity that we must take advantage of.

Let us shine the light of Christ so brightly on these social networks that all will come to see and know the love of God through our conversations online.

It's my prayer that this book becomes a resource to you in furthering your ministry efforts, both in your local context that you serve and in the global context that we're all finding ourselves in with today's technology.

APPENDIX

ONLINE ACCOUNTABILITY

People are often afraid of the Internet, and for good reason. Before social media became the number one activity on the Web, the highest traffic source online was pornography. We also hear of many extramarital affairs that are initiated on social networks. There are **two very good safeguards that I recommend** you implement that can protect you and your family while online.

First, use an accountability software program on your computer and mobile devices. Find some great resources at XXXchurch.com, such as x3watch.com for accountability; or use Safe Eyes (internetsafety.com) filtering software to protect your children online.

Second, share your log in information to *all* social networks with your spouse and an accountability partner.

ONLINE ADVERTISING

There are many great and affordable online advertising options for the church. In the past, advertising was very expensive and incredibly hard to manage. Online advertising can be easily defined and measured, making it a great option for the church or any ministry. I want to highlight three primary options.

Google Adwords: Google offers a program for nonprofits (and just opened up to religious organizations) for $10,000/month worth of free advertising. Yes, you read that correctly! You can create an ad that will allow people to find you by searching with key words such as "looking for a church in _____" or "feeling hopeless." Think about the possibilities, and start experimenting! This is a free $120,000 annual gift that Google is offering you, so please don't miss out on this opportunity! Go to google.com/nonprofits and get started today.

Facebook ads: This is where I started with online advertising and is still my preference (even though they do not give us free ads). You can specifically target an audience and use pictures to capture their attention, and there are many options for various types of ads, from sponsored stories to external links. To get started with Facebook advertising, go to facebook.com/advertising/ and get to know the platform and get started. Experiment, experiment, experiment!

You can start by setting a daily budget of $5 and increase it as you feel that your advertising dollars are being spent effectively.

LinkedIn ads: I don't advise you to invest any time on these. In my experience, they are expensive and ineffective. The minimum CPC (cost per click) bid that you can set is $2, which is ridiculously expensive. This advertising platform is only effective for businesses seeking to target very specific clients. I share this because I am often asked about using these.

Online advertising tip: One of the key measurement tools with online advertising is your CTR (click-through rate). If you have a CTR of over 1%, you have a very effective ad. This also means that when you pay on a CPC (cost per click) rate, if you are paying 25 cents CPC, for every $1 spent, four people followed your link and over 400 people saw your ad on their computer screen. That's amazing exposure at such a very low cost!

E-MAIL MARKETING/NEWSLETTERS

E-mail is not dead and is one of the most direct forms of communication you can use. Many of the e-mail marketing platforms that exist today have great social media integration and can be a very good addition to your social media strategy. Building an e-mail database will cost you little and has great value.

Here are some great e-mail marketing platforms:

Mail Chimp (mailchimp.com)

This is one of the hottest e-mail marketing platforms out there right now and has a great feature for smaller organizations, where you can have up to 2,000 e-mail addresses in your database and use the system for FREE! Mail Chimp is a great place to start!

Constant Contact (constantcontact.com)

This is the platform that I use for CBC Online and prefer. It has the greatest number of features and functionality of all of the platforms that I have found, as well as great training materials in how to use e-mail marketing effectively.

BombBomb (bombbomb.com)

This is a great new platform that many churches are using, as it integrates with the FellowshipONE church database system. It also specializes in video email, which many people are finding to be very effective.

> (!) **Ministry Tip**—Children's Ministry
>
> E-mail is a great way to communicate with parents, but don't let the communication line stop with this one-way communication line. Make sure you link your parents to your ministry's Facebook group or page, and ⟶

create an ongoing dialogue. This will not only allow you to connect with them personally but also establishes a way for parents to connect with each other. You will be surprised at how well parents can minister to each other simply by your opening up a communication platform for them to connect. Opening up these communication channels also provides a great way to communicate ministry needs and recruit new volunteers.

COPYRIGHTS

There are so many opinions regarding copyright laws and how it affects churches/nonprofits that you can probably justify almost anything. My suggestion, though, is that if you think you might be violating a copyright law, you probably are. Without written permission to use a song, video, picture, or any kind of content that you did not create, you are likely violating these laws either intentionally or unintentionally. While this might cause you more work, following the laws of the land is always a good idea!

MEDIA RELEASE FOR MINORS

You cannot post pictures or videos of minors without parental permission. Whether you are a small church or a very large ministry, this applies to everyone! Legally, you cannot show any "recognizable" photo of a child, which means that you can post a photo from the back of a head or if their face is blurred. The best practice is always to protect yourself and the children in your ministry by having written permission from the parents of every minor whose picture you might show on your website or on any social network.

At Community Bible Church, we include this on the back of our first-time registration forms for children and double-check that we have it on file before posting any photo online. I also encourage you to renew this release form on an annual basis with each minor involved in your ministry. Below is an example of a simple media release form that you might consider using.

I hereby grant permission for [church or ministry name] to record pictures or videos of my child [minor's name] while on the church property or at a church-sponsored event. I also give permission to [church or ministry name] to use these images or videos in church print and online publications (including church websites and social networks).

_____

Parent/guardian signature and date

_____

Parent/guardian name (please print)

ABOUT THE AUTHOR

PERSONAL INFORMATION

Nils Smith is the social media pastor at Community Bible Church in San Antonio, Texas. In July 2010, Nils helped to launch the CBC Online community that has grown to over 10,000 in weekly online worship attendance, with services in both English and Spanish. CBC Online has also expanded into launching Online LifeGroups and has an active Facebook community of over 200,000 people from all over the world.

Nils graduated from Texas State University with a bachelor degree in business administration and also holds a master's in ministry leadership from Rockbridge Seminary. He has been married to wife Katie for 8 years, and they have two beautiful girls together—Emery and Shelby.

CHURCH CONSULTING AND COACHING

Nils Smith has had the privilege of working with some incredible churches and ministries across the country and would love to work with you and your church as a consultant or coach. Here are some of the areas that Nils has helped both businesses and ministries thrive in:

- Advertising strategies (Google Adwords and Facebook ads)
- Social media goal setting and strategy development
- Social media coaching
- Measuring analytics and goals
- E-mail marketing
- Online church systems
- Overall Web strategies.

You can find Nils online at NilsSmith.com or on Twitter @NilsSmith.